Grumpy Old Git Jokes

This edition published in the United Kingdom in 2015 by
Portico
1 Gower Street
London
WC1E 6HD

An imprint of Pavilion Books Company Limited

ISBN 978-1-909396-75-3

A CIP catalogue record for this book is available from the British Library.

10 9 8 7 6 5 4 3

Printed and bound by Bookwell, Finland

This book can be ordered direct from the publisher at www.pavilionbooks.com.

Grumpy Old Git Jokes

Ian Allen

PORTICO

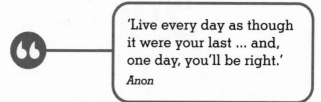

'Live every day as though it were your last ... and, one day, you'll be right.'
Anon

Bah, humbug!

 'Always start the day with a smile – you might as well get it over with early.'

Anon

We ought to feel sorry for grumpy old gits – they haven't always been like that, you know. Granted, most of them have always been grumpy – grumpy baby, grumpy kid, grumpy dad, now grumpy old git. They reckon that if you're always miserable you won't be quite so disappointed when life dumps on you from a great height, as it frequently does.

So, how do you spot a grumpy old git when you're going about your daily life? To be honest, it isn't difficult: permanent scowl; vocabulary consisting solely of 'tut!'; mistrust of anything new, young or different – if you see someone correcting a grocer's apostrophe with a marker pen, it's definitely a grumpy old git.

In this book you'll find a collection of some of the things that really get their goat, and a few sentences explaining why from a typical grumpy old git we bumped into – he wasn't very happy about that, as you can imagine. We could have completely filled the book with their ramblings about stuff that annoys them, but that would have been far too depressing, so we've chucked in a collection of jokes on all the themes that irritate them the most, not that there's any chance it will cheer up your average GOG. Some things do bring a thin smile to their sour faces, though. They like a bit of slapstick now and again; as Mel Brooks once said,

'Tragedy is when I cut my finger, comedy is when you fall into an open sewer and die.' And the shortest joke in the world is in fact a grumpy old git joke:

Knock, knock.

Get lost!

But as there aren't enough grumpy jokes around to stop you all going off and throwing yourself under a bus in despair, you'll find all sorts of gags in the following pages. A wise man once said, 'To steal from one man is plagiarism, but to steal from many is research,' and this book is packed full of well-researched jokes.

Some people say, 'There's no point to life without laughter,' and might generously think that the following jokes have been added not to pad out the book, but to deliberately counterpoint the grumpy theme and affirm that the world isn't such a bad old place, after all. A grumpy old git would just say, 'There's no point to life,' and add that life is an extended hostage situation that no one's getting out of alive.

So, if you're a grumpy old git, read this book to reaffirm all your old prejudices and bugbears. And if you're not, but just like having the occasional moan, read it as a warning to what you might turn into if you're not careful!

'Think how stupid the average person is, and realise half of them are stupider than that.'

George Carlin

'If I'd known I was going to live this long I'd have taken better care of myself.'
Eubie Blake

Old People

Old people really make me mad: old drivers on the roads, pensioners pushing supermarket trolleys at five miles a fortnight, old farts paying for everything in loose change ('You don't mind a bit of shrapnel, do you, love?'). Let's be clear – just because I'm a self-professed grumpy old git, that doesn't make me old. Old is about 15 years older than I am (and always will be, if I've got anything to do with it). And just because you're old, you don't have to be geriatric; if 70 is the new 50, then for some old codgers 80 is the new 120. It's true what they say: despite the high cost of living, it's still very popular.

How am I supposed to get paid a decent enough pension in a couple of years to support my golf fees and wine club when it's all being paid out to nonagenarians so they can waste it on tea cosies and Fisherman's Friends and bread? It's as if they don't know what the cemetery's for – can't they take a hint next time they go to a funeral?

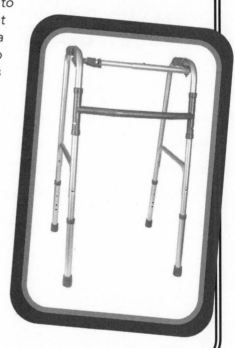

Solicitor: Would you like me to read your will back to you?
Old git: Not all of it, just the good bit where I disinherit the entire family.

First old git: I had an SUV for my birthday.
Second old git: That's handy.
First old git: *I'll* say – socks, underpants, Viagra.

First old git: I wish I knew where I was going to die.
Second old git: Why's that?
First old git: Well, I'd make sure I never went there, for a start.

Two old gits are sat on a bench in the garden of the old folks' home when another resident runs past with no clothes on.

'Was that Mabel?' asked one of them.

'Yes,' said the other, 'but what was she wearing?'

'God knows, but it needed a good iron.'

Old git: Doctor, I keep forgetting to zip up my flies – am I going senile?

Doctor: No, don't worry, senility is when you forget to unzip them.

A party of pensioners is on a coach trip to the seaside, and every so often they pass a dish of nuts forward to the driver. As they're getting off he thanks them for the nuts, but says,

'Are you sure you had enough for yourselves?'

'Oh yes,' said one, 'we can only suck the chocolate off them at our age anyway.'

Old git: Why are you spending £20 on face cream?

Wife: It's to make me look younger. You're spending money on beer, aren't you?

Old git: Yes, but for a tenner, I can get more than enough beer to make you look younger.

Two old gits were chatting in the front room while their wives were in the kitchen, and one old git told the other about a nice pub they'd been to recently.

'What was it called?' asked his friend.

'Oh, hang on, erm, I can't remember ... what's the name of that nice-smelling flower in the garden, lots of thorns?'

'Rose?'

'That's it! Rose,' he shouted to his wife, 'what was the name of that pub we went to last week?

How do you make a little old lady swear?

Get another little old lady to shout 'Bingo!'

> **First old git: Windy, isn't it?**
>
> Second old git: No, Thursday.
>
> **First old git: So am I, let's go to the pub.**

Two really old gits were driving to the pub.
After they'd passed through three red lights
on the trot, the one in the passenger seat said,
'I wish you'd be a bit more careful.'
'Sorry,' said the other, 'I thought you were driving.'

Two old gits go to a solicitor to make their wills.
'Right,' says the solicitor, 'who wants to go first?'

An old couple were out for dinner and after a while the old lady went to the bathroom. A younger woman came over to the old man and said, 'Excuse me, are you and that lady married?'

'Sixty-five years,' he replied.

'That's wonderful, and I notice all the time you're calling her "sweetheart", "love" and "darling". That's so romantic.'

'Well,' said the old chap, 'to tell the truth, I forgot what her name was about ten years ago...'

Jimmy: My granddad beat my granny to death yesterday.

Teacher: That's awful, Jimmy. Is he under arrest?

Jimmy: No, I mean he died and she's still alive.

Just before the funeral service, the undertaker came up to the very elderly widow and asked, 'How old was your husband?'

'Ninety-eight,' she replied. 'Two years older than me.'

'So you're ninety-six,' the undertaker commented.

'Yes, hardly worth me going home, is it?'

A doctor was checking three old gits at the old folks' home.

'What's five times five?' he asked the first one.

'Seven hundred.'

'What's three times three?' he asked the second one.

'Bananas,' came the reply.

In desperation he asked the last one, 'What's two times two?'

'Four.'

'Finally!' said the doctor. 'Well done. How did you work that out?'

'It was easy,' said the last old git. 'I just subtracted bananas from seven hundred.'

'I once shot an elephant in my pyjamas. How he got into my pyjamas I'll never know.'

Groucho Marx

Animals

Animals – apart from the delicious ones – are vastly overrated. The ones that aren't big enough and nasty enough to want to kill you and eat you given half a chance would happily take a crafty nibble out of your liver if they came across your inert body lying in the street, rather than calling for an ambulance or starting CPR like a civilised human being would. 'Ah, but animals don't make war,' you'll be told by those budgie-cuddlers who'd cheerfully demolish a perfectly good old folks' home or pub to make way for a donkey sanctuary. Well, the slugs have certainly declared war on my vegetable patch, and if I could I'd nuke the lot of 'em. You see, I don't mind animals as long as they stay in their territory (i.e. the farm, then the abattoir, then the butcher's) and keep out of mine, by which I mean no mice in my house, no pests in my garden, no cats fighting outside my bedroom in the middle of the night, and definitely no dog poo between my house and the pub. Fair enough.

> **What do you call a moth who hates light?**
> A Goth moth.

An old git was driving in a country lane when he drove into a ditch. Luckily, a farmer was passing by with a horse and offered to pull him out. 'Me and old Captain will have you out in no time,' he said. So they attached a rope between Captain and the car and the farmer shouted, 'Pull, Neddy ... Pull, Clover ... Pull, Captain.'

And at that the horse pulled the car out of the ditch.

'Thanks,' said the old git, 'but why did you use those other names?'

'Well, Captain is a bit lazy, but he's blind. He'd never have pulled you out if he'd thought he was doing it by himself.'

How do you hire a horse?
Put a brick under each hoof.

First flamingo: My kids are really naughty at the moment.
Second flamingo: Well, you should put your foot down.

Zoo visitor: Why is the monkey enclosure empty?
Zookeeper: It's the mating season, they're inside.
Visitor: Do you think they'd come out for peanuts?
Zookeeper: Would you?

**How do you make
a bull sweat?**
Give him a
tight jersey.

What did the slug
say to the snail?

'Big Issue?'

Old git: I've killed seven flies this morning, five males and two females.

Wife: How do you know what sex they were?

Old git: Five were on the beer can and two were on the phone.

How do bats navigate without bumping into things?

They use their wing mirrors.

First old git: I threw a hedgehog at a dartboard the other day.

Second old git: What happened?

First old git: I scored 1,354.

There was a rabbit who went to a café every day and ordered either a cheese toastie or a ham toastie. One day he decided to go mad and ordered one of each. But it was too much for his little bunny tummy and he died.

When he got to rabbit heaven, St Peter Rabbit asked him, 'What killed you?'

And the rabbit replied... 'Mixing my toasties.'

First old git: I collect badgers.

Second old git: Have you got many?

First old git: I just need one more for the whole sett.

What do you call a woodpecker without a beak?

A head-banger.

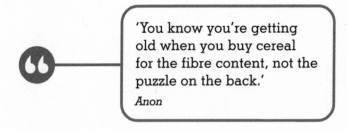

'You know you're getting old when you buy cereal for the fibre content, not the puzzle on the back.'

Anon

Supermarkets

Supermarkets really used to be super 30 or 40 years ago. They gave you an option. You'd go to town and would either potter from shop to shop collecting what you required as you went, or whizz round the new-fangled 'super' market, which was a largish but manageable store that had a reasonable selection of most of what you needed, and some of what you didn't. You might go to the supermarket one week and the specialist shops the next. You had a choice. Not any more. Supermarkets are now typically the size of Stoke and just as inspiring, and you need a satnav to find your way round. The staff are hand-picked for their ability to say 'dunno' without moving their lips, and their idea of helping with your packing is to put your 12-pack of Ruddles on top of your soft sliced loaf. And if you decide to go to your local town centre for shopping instead, don't bother. They've all closed down thanks to the supermarkets. (Not that I've used the town centre lately myself, much too expensive, ruddy rip-off merchants … still, it'd be nice to have the choice.)

Supermarket manager: Welcome to the store, young man. Your first job is to sweep up.

New recruit: But I'm a university graduate!

Manager: Oh, I'm sorry, I didn't realise. Well, this thing here is called a 'broom'. I'll show you how to use it.

Checkout operator: I bet you're single, aren't you?

Old git: Yes, I am. Is it that obvious from what I'm buying?

Checkout operator: No, you're just really ugly.

Old git: Excuse me, this lane is marked 'eight items or fewer', can't you read?

Young git: Yes, but I can't count.

Shopper: Do these frozen
chickens get any bigger?

Assistant: No, they're all dead.

**Shopper: Can I exchange these two bags of
raisins for sultanas, please?**
Assistant: Yes, but I can only give you one bag
of sultanas for them.
Shopper: Why's that?
Assistant: That's the currant exchange rate.

What shop sells
right-angled
triangles?

Pythag-R-Us.

A supermarket manager overheard an assistant telling a customer, 'No, we haven't had any in for ages and it doesn't look like we'll be getting any more.'

Enraged, the manager interrupted and told the shopper, 'Don't take any notice of him, madam. I personally placed an order only yesterday and they'll be here in a few days.'

The shopper left looking puzzled and the manager said to the assistant, 'Never, never tell a customer we don't have something. Now, what was she asking after?'

'Well, you remember when we had those tarantulas in the bananas...'

First old git: My new wife's a big disappointment.

Second old git: How come?

First old git: Well, when she said she was 'experienced in the bedroom department', it turned out she'd been working at IKEA for 15 years.

> **Customer: Do you have any OXO cubes?**
> Assistant: No, sir, we're out of stock.

Why is customer service better in the US?
Because there, the underlying principle is that the customer is always … carrying a gun.

First old git: That specialist Polish shop I opened has gone bust.
Second old git: I'd have thought it would have done really well, nowadays.
First old git: You'd have thought so, but apparently there's only so much Mr Sheen and Pledge people can use.

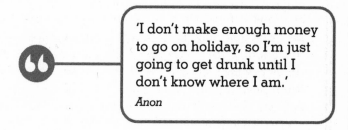

'I don't make enough money to go on holiday, so I'm just going to get drunk until I don't know where I am.'

Anon

Holidays

Holidays. What a nightmare. I'll start by assuming you're not going with children, because if you are it doesn't matter where in the world you go, it'll be an utter disaster; your choice is between a merely expensive disaster and an utterly exorbitant, credit-busting, eviction-threatening disaster. Take your pick. Turning to holidays sans children, you can either go abroad or stay in the UK. If you go foreign your trip will be blighted by striking French air-traffic controllers, overzealous US customs officials and a combination of unpleasant diseases that only flourish in the tropics. If you stay in this country your break will be ruined by traffic jams, other people's children and, of course, the weather. Alternatively, you could actually stay at your own home and go for 'days out' to various decaying historic properties in your area that will be free of kids. This is no better: firstly, for the money it will cost you to get into our stately homes you could have flown to Florida; secondly, these places are clear of juveniles because they are so ruddy BORING; and thirdly, if you're at home for the week Mrs Old-Git will immediately think of several 'little jobs' that need doing around the house. Frankly, you'd have more of a rest and be a lot better off staying at work...

> **Holiday-maker: I'm looking for something cheap and nasty to take home for my mother-in-law.**
>
> Souvenir shop owner: Hang on and you can take my father-in-law.

First old git: They ruined all my luggage at the airport.

Second old git: Did you get any compensation?

First old git: No, they said I didn't have much of a case.

First old git: I'm going to the Virgin Islands this year.

Second old git: Why's that?

First old git: Well, last year I went to the Canary Islands and I never saw a single canary...

Where do you go for a cheap UK holiday?
The Off-Peak District.

Did you hear about the man who went swimming on holiday in Australia when the shark-warning flags were flying?
It cost him an arm and a leg.

First old git: My wife's just swum the Channel.
Second old git: Good for her.
First old git: Of course, I was supporting her all the way, shouting encouragement from a megaphone on the boat. She still reckons we could have afforded another ferry ticket.

Man: How would you like to go on a round-the-world holiday?
Wife: I'd rather go somewhere else.

First old git: Did you enjoy your seaside holiday?
Second old git: It was such a dump, even the tide didn't bother coming back.

An old git was checking in his luggage.
'I'd like this one to go to Rotterdam, and this one to Madrid,' he said.
'But you're going to Florida, sir, we just can't do that.'
'Why not, you did last year.'

First old git: That Punch and Judy show at the end of the pier was the worst I've ever seen.
Second old git: When I saw it this morning it was at the middle of the pier. Are you sure it was the end of the pier?
First old git: Positive. I've just set fire to it.

Old tourist: Have you saved many people this summer?
Lifeguard: Dozens.
Old tourist: And have you saved any young women?
Lifeguard: Quite a few.
Old tourist: Can I have one?

Horace was on holiday in Australia and decided to take a train trip. He was queuing behind a young lady who, when it was her turn, requested, 'Alice Springs, single.'
When it was his turn, he said, 'Horace Perkins, married.'
'Where do you want to go?' the attendant asked.
'None of your business,' he said, 'you didn't ask Alice Springs.'

First old git: My wife went on a pony-trekking holiday this year in an attempt to lose weight.
Second old git: Did it work?
First old git: Not really, but the pony lost three stone.

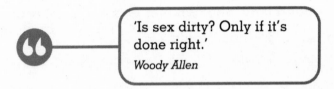

'Is sex dirty? Only if it's done right.'
Woody Allen

Sex

To hear young people go on about sex nowadays you'd think they invented it. In fact, they spend so much time watching it, analysing it and talking about it, I'd be surprised if any of them actually found the time to get round to doing it. It's everywhere except where it should be, and that's in private. You can't switch the TV on without seeing breasts bursting out of tops and buttocks bobbing up and down suggestively ... and that's just Strictly Come Dancing. I'm fully expecting a new dance to be introduced for the next series: 'All right, my loves? And now we have the lovely, voluptuous Ola and her celebrity partner Jeremy Paxman, and they will be performing the Twerk.' And you certainly can't go near the Internet without asking for trouble. I was looking for pictures of North American wildlife the other day, and it got very embarrassing when Mrs Old-Git walked in as I was searching for cougars, I can tell you...

Woman: Gosh, your willy's shaped like a pepper grinder.

Man: I'll take that as a condiment.

Two old gits open a pub. After six months and hardly any customers one says, 'Let's close the pub and open a brothel.'

'Don't be stupid,' says the other. 'If we can't sell beer, how are we going to sell broth?'

Old git: I want a full medical. I'm getting married next week to a 22-year-old model.

Doctor: But you're 94. I have to warn you it could prove fatal.

Old git: If she dies, she dies.

Two old gits are getting changed in the leisure centre. One takes his trousers off to reveal a set of tights.

'How long have you been wearing tights?' his mate asks.

'**Ever since my wife found a pair in the back of the car...**'

Have you heard of the new condoms coated in French liqueur?

They're called Cointreauceptives.

Why does it take a million sperm to fertilise one egg?

None of them will stop to ask for directions.

Woman: Doctor, I've forgotten to take my contradictive pills.

Doctor: Are you ignorant?

Woman: Yes, three months.

Date: You said on your profile you were skinny, but you must weigh 20 stone.

Old git: Yes, but I've got lots of skin...

Man in chemist: Ten Durex, please, miss.

Middle-aged chemist: Don't 'miss' me, young man.

Man: OK then, make it eleven.

> **A chicken and an egg are lying in bed together.**
>
> The chicken lights a cigarette and says, 'Well, that answers that question.'

First old git: When did you last have sex?

Second old git: 1955.

First old git: Crikey, that's a long time.

Second old git: Not really, it's only 21:20 now.

'The English, the English, the English are best, I wouldn't give tuppence for all of the rest.'

Flanders and Swann

Foreigners

I don't mind foreigners as long as they accept they'll never be as good as us English. But they all look down their noses at us nowadays – how the Aussies have the nerve, I don't know – and even though our entry is always every bit as rubbish as everyone else's, we've got about as much chance of winning the Eurovision Song Contest as I have of becoming Pope ... just because they all hate us. And every damn programme on TV seems to be American, and they can't even speak English properly – we are certainly 'two nations divided by a common language', as George Bernard Shaw may or may not have said. Anyway, the only consolation we can take while we're being beaten by other countries at all the games we invented, is that at least we can have a good laugh at them...

> **What do you call a sheep tied to a lamppost in Melbourne?**
>
> A leisure centre.

Why did the Italian chicken cross the road?
To surrender to the other side.

Old lady: Is there anything worn under the kilt?
Scotsman: No, it's all in perfect working order.

What do you call a Welshman in the football World Cup Final?
'Ref!'

How do you get rid of German aristocrats?
Von by Von.

Why do the French eat snails?
They don't like fast food.

What happens when a New Zealander goes to live in Australia?
The average IQ of both countries goes up.

What's the difference between Australia and yogurt?
A yogurt has culture.

Old git: Three pounds of potatoes, please.
Grocer: Sorry, we only sell kilos now we're in Europe.
Old git: Oh right, well, three pounds of kilos then.

How many Spaniards does it take to change a light bulb?

Just Juan.

Australian immigration officer: What's the purpose of your visit to Australia?

Englishman: Holiday.

Officer: Do you have any criminal convictions?

Englishman: I didn't know you still needed one.

Why are Englishmen so good at rowing?

Because you get to sit down and go backwards.

How did the Italian chef die?

He pasta way.

Why do Italian men grow moustaches?

To look like their mothers.

> **What do you call a sophisticated American?**
>
> A Canadian.

How do we know Adam was an Englishman?
Who else would stand beside a naked woman and be tempted by an apple?

How do you get 20 Argentinians inside a telephone box?
Tell them it belongs to someone else.

How many Scotsmen does it take to change a light bulb?
'Och, it's not that dark.'

What happened to the Dutchman with inflatable shoes?
He popped his clogs.

If you spin an old Chinese man round and round, does he become disoriented?

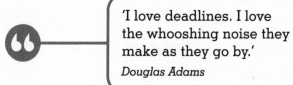

'I love deadlines. I love
the whooshing noise they
make as they go by.'
Douglas Adams

Working for a Living

Philip Larkin once compared work to a toad, squatting over our lives, making us all miserable. And if that doesn't sound like the loveable old Larkin you know, you're probably thinking of the jolly David Jason character from The Darling Buds of May, not the dusty old librarian of Hull University. Far be it for me to correct a bloke who was offered the poet laureateship, and a fellow grumpy old git to boot, but surely a toad's a bit on the light side? I would say work is more like an elephant or a hippopotamus, something you definitely don't want to get squashed by. There are some people who love their work, true, and they are known as 'annoying'. They swan around the office with an 'aren't we lucky to work here?' look on their face, and it's a miracle I've got to my age without impaling a gross of them on the end of a javelin. Oscar Wilde had it right when he said, 'Work is the curse of the drinking classes.' And anything that keeps me out of the pub has got to be a bad idea.

Interviewer: What is your worst quality?

Job applicant: Honesty.

Interviewer: I don't think honesty is a bad quality.

Job applicant: I don't care what you think, you ugly old git.

An old git took his boots to a cobbler's and said, 'I want these soled.'

He went back the next day and asked for his boots.

'Oh,' said the cobbler, 'Here's a fiver, I've sold them.'

Dentist: That's the biggest cavity I've ever seen, the biggest cavity I've ever seen.

Old git: There's no need to repeat yourself.

Dentist: I didn't, that was an echo.

Interviewer: What makes you think you're suitable to work as a night watchman?
Old git: Well, the least little noise wakes me up.

Interviewer: Describe yourself in three words.
Applicant: Very bad at maths.

Road worker: The shovels haven't arrived for the job yet – what should we do?
Foreman: You'll just have to lean on one another until they turn up.

First interviewer: Do you think that last chap could do the job as an insect-packer?
Second interviewer: Well, he certainly boxed all the right ticks.

What do you need to get a job in Australia?

Good koalafications.

Why did the diplomat's bath keep ringing?
His tap had been phoned.

A man fell from the second floor of a hotel onto the pavement below and lay spread-eagled and concussed. A porter ran out of the lobby and went to his side.
'What happened?' he asked.
'You tell me, I've only just got here.'

The boss walked in on an employee kissing his secretary. 'Is this what we pay you for?' he shouted.

'No,' said the man, 'I do this for free.'

Old git: I start a new job on Monday, with 500 men under me.

Wife: You? Never! What's the job?

Old git: Cutting the grass at the cemetery.

Safety inspector: If there was an explosion in the boilerhouse and your colleague was blown into the air, what would you do first?

Old git: I'd wait for him to come down.

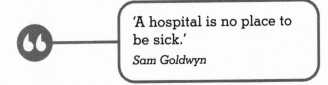

'A hospital is no place to be sick.'

Sam Goldwyn

Hospitals and Health

The older we get, the more obsessed we are with our health. Everything starts to pack in: joints, bones, organs, brains ... it's only the old codgers keeping the NHS in business. Thank God for smokers, I say, paying all that tax on every packet of fags they buy, funding a health service they'll probably never get to use – they should give 'em all a medal if you ask me. Hospitals are depressing places at the best of times but, let's face it, the older you get, the less chance you've got of getting out of one alive. If you're a patient you get prodded, poked and have cold, unfriendly instruments inserted into every orifice. And even if you're only visiting, chances are you'll catch some ghastly skin-eating virus from some lazy git who can't be bothered to wash his hands...

Doctor: I'm sorry to tell you that you have cancer.

Old git: Oh no, that's awful.

Doctor: And also, you appear to have Alzheimer's.

Old git: Well, it could be worse – at least I don't have cancer.

A new doctor at a hospital was chatting to colleagues when a fat man in a suit rushed through the ward shouting, 'Typhoid! Tetanus! MMR! Diptheria!'

'Who on earth was that?' he asked when the man had gone.

'Oh, he's the finance director,' said another doctor. 'He calls the shots around here.'

Doctor: I've had your test results back and your white blood count is elevated.

Old git: What does that mean?

Doctor: It means it's up.

> **Doctor: All you've got is hypochondria.**
> Patient: Can you give me anything for it?

Old git: Doctor, ever since you operated on my wife she's lost interest in sleeping with me.
Doctor: All we did was remove her cataracts.

Doctor: Why have you discharged Mrs Anderson?
Nurse: We had a memo saying there was no place on the ward for Mrs A.
Doctor: You idiot, that said MRSA!

What happened to the man who was hit by a train and lost his left arm, leg, ear and eye?
He's all right now.

Nurse: Hello, Ward 7.

Old git: Can you tell me how Mr Edwards is doing after his operation, please?

Nurse: He's doing very well, responding positively and should be allowed out in a couple of days. Are you a close family member?

Old git: No, I'm Mr Edwards. Nobody here will tell me anything.

Things you don't want to overhear in the operating theatre:

'No, nurse, I said remove his *spectacles*.'

'Better save that, we might need it for the post-mortem.'

'Has anyone seen my watch?'

Nurse: Doctor, the patient you've just treated has dropped dead on the step as he was leaving. What should I do?
Doctor: Turn him round so it looks like he was coming in.

Surgeon: Now this patient has a bad limp because of the deformity in his leg. What would you do in a case like this?
Medical student: Erm, I think I'd limp as well.

Was my operation a success, doctor?
Er, I'm not a doctor, I'm St Peter.

Old git: This suppository must have come from IKEA.
Second old git: Why do you say that?
Old git: Because I've got to put it up myself.

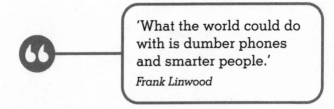

'What the world could do
with is dumber phones
and smarter people.'
Frank Linwood

Technology

I know what they're up to, and have been for years. It's called built-in obsolescence and it's costing everyone a fortune. Most of the gadgets and devices we were using 10 or 15 years ago were perfectly all right. We had a little phone we could take anywhere and, guess what, we could use it to make phone calls. Now a phone has to run your life; I'm surprised nobody's married theirs yet. TVs are another thing. I had a lovely colour telly in 1990, great picture, still going strong. A couple of years ago Mrs Old-Git decided we needed a new one the size of Jodrell Bank. Why?! Every gadget is the same: bigger, smaller, louder ... more things to go wrong. Imagine if the same principle applied to houses. 'What? You're still living in a semi-detached 3.1? That's not compatible with anything now, you'll have to knock it down and upgrade. We won't be supporting your house after 2015 anyway.' Ruddy rip-off, all of it.

> Did you hear about the mean old git who bought his grandson an Etch-a-Sketch and told him it was an iPad?

A man using Apple Maps walks into a bar.
Or maybe a shop ... or an optician's ... or perhaps a church.

There's a new device to let Apple users greet each other.
The iFive.

Salesman: Let me assure you, with our printers, failure is not an option.
Old git: No, it seems to come as standard.

Why are computers like air conditioners?
They work fine until you start opening Windows.

Why did the man Ohm marry the lady Ohm?
He couldn't resistor.

Computer hierarchy:
Son: iPod
Daughter: iPhone
Mum: iPad
Dad: iPay

Why did the computer geek burn his mouth?
He ate pizza before it was cool.

Old git: Why is there reggae music coming from my printer?
Helpline: Don't worry, that's just the paper jamming.

Customer: There's something wrong with my laptop. It keeps playing 'Skyfall' constantly.
Technician: Sounds like your computer is a Dell.

Old git: I knew I was unpopular, but the last straw was when I got in the car yesterday.

Second old git: How's that?

First old git: Even the satnav has stopped talking to me.

How many computer programmers does it take to change a light bulb?

None, it's a hardware problem.

First old git: I wish I hadn't changed the voice in my Satnav to Bonnie Tyler.

Second old git: Why's that?

First old git: Well, now it keeps telling me to turn around all the time, and every now and then it falls apart.

What happened when the man dropped his iPad in the river?

It started synching.

An old git was finally persuaded to have a mobile phone. He was trudging round Lidl when it went off for the first time. It was his wife.

'I'm just testing your phone,' she said. 'Isn't the reception good?'

'I suppose so,' said her husband, 'but how did you know I was in Lidl?'

Doris: I got sacked for having dyslexia.

Doreen: They can't do that. What happened?

Doris: It turns out the boss wanted me to unzip his files.

Youth: I've got Google+, Facebook and Twitter.

Old git: What you need is a life.

Youth: OK, can you send me a link?

IT guy: What version of Windows do you have installed?

Old git: Double-glazed.

'A man is never drunk if he can lie on the floor without holding on.'

Joe E. Lewis

Drinking

Drinking used to be very simple. You would pop in the pub for a pint with your lunch, then have a swift one on the way home. A sherry before dinner, a bottle of wine with your meal and a couple of large whiskies before bed. Everything in moderation. But now, because some folk like to get bladdered in public, start a punch-up with the boys in blue and then regurgitate everything they've drunk into the gutter, alcohol is not only being taxed to high heaven (which should give the chunder-junkies something to think about it – they're throwing up about 50 per cent tax), but it's now the business of every man and his dog how much we all drink. I can't even go to the dentist without him asking me how many 'units' I drink a week. I'd like to tell him to mind his own ruddy business, but that's never a good thing to say to someone who's about to stick a drill in your mouth. To me, a unit is what something comes in. So, one bottle of wine – one unit; one bottle of whisky – one unit; one barrel of beer ... well, you get the idea. This seems to satisfy my dentist, anyway.

> **Barman: That's a dreadful case of the shakes you've got. You must drink a lot.**
>
> Old git: Not really, I spill most of it.

Two men are chatting at the bar.
'Where are you from?' asks one.
'Ireland.'
'So am I. What city?'
'Cork.'
'No kidding? So am I. What school did you go to?'
'St Patrick's, I left in 1998.'
'That's incredible, so did I.'
The barman, watching all this, remarks to another customer, 'I see the O'Malley twins are drunk again.'

Barman: Bitter?
Old git: No, just fed up.

One tequila, two tequila, three tequila, floor.

An old git faints in a pub and comes round just as they're loosening his shirt and fanning his face.

'What happened?' he asks.

'It's all right,' says his friend, 'we've just brought you to.'

'If you have I don't remember. You'd better bring me two more.'

A policeman approaches a drunk walking down the road pulling a piece of string with a loop on the end of it.

'Have you seen the invisible man?' asks the drunk.

'No,' said the policeman, humouring him. 'Why?'

'I've found his dog.'

Youth: Give me a beer, please.

Barmaid: You're only 16. Do you want to get me into trouble?

Youth: Later, maybe, but now I just want a beer.

First drunk: Do you know what the time is?
Second drunk: Yes.
First drunk: Thanks.

Wife: Why do you call my mother 'The Exorcist'?
Old git: Have you noticed how quickly the spirits
disappear when she's here?

**A old git goes in a pub and orders nine pints of
lager. When they're all set up he drinks the first,
third, fifth, seventh and ninth then goes to leave.**
'Hey,' said the barman, 'aren't you going to have
these?'
**'I can't,' said the man, 'my doctor told me I could
only have the odd drink.'**

Two old gits are in a pub.
One says, 'Your round.'

The other says, 'You can talk, fatty.'

What happened when a woman went into a pub and asked the barman for a double entendre?
He gave her one.

A woman is lying in bed when she hears her husband come in from the pub. There follows much crashing and banging.
'What the hell do you think you're doing?' she finally shouts.
'I'm trying to get a gallon of beer upstairs.'
'Don't be so stupid. For God's sake leave it downstairs.'
'I can't, I've drunk it.'

Barman: Why have you got a pork pie on your head?
Old git: I always have a pork pie on my head on a Tuesday.
Barman: But today's Wednesday.
Old git: What?! I must look like a right idiot.

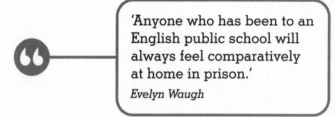

'Anyone who has been to an English public school will always feel comparatively at home in prison.'

Evelyn Waugh

Police and Authority

The British police are the best in the world, they say. Well, the best at doling out speeding tickets, perhaps, or prosecuting you for giving some tearaway a slap on the head (I didn't know he was only six – he was big for his age!). In the good old days it was them dishing out clips round the ears. You never see a policeman now ... and if a cop car goes past with its lights and sirens on, chances are they're just trying to get back to the station before the fish and chips go cold. Everyone with a bit of authority is the same, mind ... give them a bit of power and it goes straight to their heads. If it isn't judges letting off criminals because they come from a broken home (course it is – they ruddy broke it!) it's magistrates having to resign for being caught with their hand in somebody's till or their trousers round their ankles. I sometimes think the anarchists have got the right idea.

Policeman: Where did you get that
'Caution – Wide Load' sign?
Man: It fell off the back of a lorry.

Constable: This is a puzzle, sarge. A large bag has just been handed in with a label saying '221B Baker Street'.
Sergeant: Sounds like a case for Sherlock Holmes.

Police in Liverpool have announced that they've found a huge stash of drugs, weapons and stolen property in a warehouse behind Toxteth Library. A local resident commented, 'Everyone round here is in a state of shock,' adding, 'we never knew we had a library.'

How many policemen does it take to change a light bulb?
None, the new bulb turned itself in.

> **Policeman: I'm booking you for dangerous driving. You were swerving all over the road.**
>
> Old Motorist: But there were nails all over the road – I couldn't drive over them.
>
> **Policeman: In that case, I'm arresting you for tacks evasion.**

What happened to the shoplifter's son?
He took after his father.

Judge: I thought I said I never wanted to see you in my court again.
Defendant: I tried to tell the police that, your honour, but they wouldn't listen.

Policeman: Didn't you hear my sirens? I could hardly catch you, you were doing over 90mph. Unless you can give me a good reason I'll have to book you.

Old motorist: Well, you see, my wife ran away with a policeman last week, and I thought you were him trying to bring her back.

Why was the kitchen installer sent to prison?
Counter-fitting.

Sergeant: Now, as a new constable, you'll face some difficult problems. What would you do if you had to arrest your own mother?
Constable: Call for armed backup!

Policeman: Can I see your licence, sir?

Old git: I wish you lot would make your mind up. Last week you took it off me for six months, now all of a sudden you want to see it again.

A lorry driver misjudges a bridge and ends up wedged fast underneath it. A traffic jam builds up and eventually a police car arrives.

'Are you stuck?' asks the copper.

'No,' says the driver, 'I was delivering this bridge and I ran out of petrol...'

Youth in street: Have you seen a policeman anywhere round here?

Old git: No.

Youth: Good, stick 'em up and give me your money.

Old motorist: Why did you stop me for speeding when everyone else was going just as fast?

Policeman: Do you ever go fishing, sir?

Old motorist: Yes, I do actually.

Policeman: And do you catch all the fish in the river?

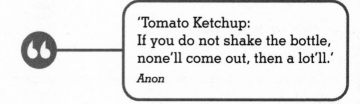

'Tomato Ketchup:
If you do not shake the bottle,
none'll come out, then a lot'll.'
Anon

Food

'How can the old git possibly be grumpy about food?' I hear you ask. Without it he'd be brown bread, and the world would be a happier place. Well, of course I eat food. I just hate certain types of food: poncy food and good-for-you food, la-di-da food and modern food, microwave food and processed food, and expensive food and suspiciously cheap food and processed food and raw food, and foreign food and fatty food and fat-free food and sugary food and sugar-free food and 'high-end' food and budget food and cordon bleu food and Gordon Bleeurgh food and all-day-breakfast food and fast food and food that takes ages to prepare and gluten-free food and allergen-free food and taste-free food and food-free food and alcohol-free food and party food and fancy food and 'traditional' food and ethnic food and experimental food and innovative food and austerity food and ... basically, I just want to be left in peace to have my dinner; and no, I'm not going to tell you what I'm having.

> **What has no beginning, no end, and a hole in the middle?**
>
> A doughnut.

Diner: Could you fetch me a cloak and a sword, please?

Waiter: I'm sorry, sir?

Diner: Well, if I'm going to have to fight this steak all night, I might as well do it properly.

First old git: I did well on the stock exchange yesterday.

Second old git: Oh really?

First old git: Yes, I swapped five Oxo cubes for a jar of Bovril.

Wife: You didn't like the fried breakfast I made you, then?

Old git: You haven't made corn flakes before, have you?

Diner: Is my table ready yet?

Maitre d': I'm afraid not, do you mind waiting?

Diner: Not at all.

Maitre d': Good, take these drinks to table four.

What happened when the fruit and veg company went into liquidation?

It was bought out by a smoothie company.

First old git: I bet my wife I could make a car out of macaroni.

Second old git: And did you?

First old git: Let's put it like this, you should have seen her face as I drove past 'er.

Man: I hope you enjoyed the meal, because I must confess I haven't got any money to pay for it!
Date: Well, I wish you'd said before. We could have gone somewhere more expensive.

Old git: You've burned the dinner again.
Wife: It's not burned, it's caramelised.
Old git: All right, you've caramelised the salad again.

First old git: Can you help me with my crossword? Seven down: 'fizzy drink', eight letters.
Second old git: I don't know ... but if it was seven up it would be lemonade.

Patient: I was cooking last night and got some herbs in my eye.

Optician: I'm afraid you're going to be parsley-sighted.

First old git: What do you do?
Second old git: I'm a spy.
First old git: But you're dressed like a farmer?
Second old git: Yes, I'm a shepherd spy.

First old git: Do you like that GM food?
Second old git: No, I think they should stick to making cars.

What do you call someone who's scared of KFC?
A chicken.

Diner: Waiter, there's a fly in my soup.
Waiter: Yes, well, the chef used to be a tailor.

'Lawyers occasionally stumble over the truth, but most of them pick themselves up and hurry off as if nothing had happened.'

Winston Churchill

Lawyers and Bankers

Who doesn't hate lawyers, bankers, solicitors ... in fact any professional whose aim in life is to separate the rest of us from our hard-earned cash by charging extortionate fees for next to no work. Bankers got so fed up of cheating us all individually for the last hundred years or so that a few years ago they decided to go for the big one and mess up the entire country collectively. And then we had to pay up and say thank you very much. And you only have to look at how many MPs are/were lawyers to see the sort of shady characters they are. As for solicitors, well you can't say good morning to one without them sending you a bill for a consultation. If the whole ruddy lot of them went on strike tomorrow nobody would notice until Christmas. And an interesting statistic is that if you pushed lawyers off Beachy Head at a rate of one every five seconds, you'd only be able to do it for ten minutes before you had to stop to wipe the tears of laughter from your eyes.

What do you need if 100 bankers are up to their necks in sand?

More sand.

The devil appears to a lawyer one night and says, 'I have an offer for you. I will make you rich, powerful, attractive to women and live in fine health to be 100. In return I ask for your soul.'

'Hmm,' says the lawyer. 'What's the catch?'

A banker is getting out of his car when another motor zooms past, taking the car door clean off. A policeman is soon on the scene to find the banker swearing and cursing.

'Look at my car – a brand-new BMW. Look at it!'

'I can't believe how materialistic you bankers are,' said the copper. 'Never mind your car, look at your arm – it's been ripped off.'

'Oh my God,' wails the banker, looking at the stump of his shoulder, 'my Rolex!'

A lawyer and a banker fall out of a plane without parachutes. The lawyer weighs 12 stone and the banker weighs 20 stone. Which one hits the ground first?

Who cares?

Research scientists in the USA have decided to use lawyers instead of rats in their experiments in future. This is because:

1 There are more lawyers than rats in the USA.

2 The scientists were sometimes reluctant to experiment on creatures they'd become attached to.

3 There are some things that rats just won't do.

Suppose you and a banker are trapped in a cage with a lion, a tiger and a leopard. You have a gun but only two bullets. What do you do?

Shoot the banker twice to make sure.

US attorney: Before you performed the autopsy, did you check the man was dead – take his pulse, check for heartbeat, etc.?

Pathologist: No.

Attorney: Why not?

Pathologist: Because his brain was sitting in a jar on my desk.

Attorney: Er, but nevertheless it's still possible he might have been alive before you began the autopsy?

Pathologist: I suppose he might have been alive and practising as an attorney somewhere.

Lawyer: Doctor, you said earlier that the victim was shot in the forest?

Doctor: No, I said he was shot in the lumbar region.

Lawyer: Now, I'm sure you're an honest and intelligent man...

Witness: Thank you. If I weren't under oath I'd return the compliment.

> **What should you throw a drowning banker?**
>
> His lawyer.

What do you call a ship full of lawyers at the bottom of the sea?
A good start.

What's the ideal weight for a banker?
About three pounds, including the urn.

What's the difference between a bad lawyer and a good lawyer?
A bad lawyer will drag out your case for months.
A good lawyer makes it last even longer.

'Christian: A man who feels repentance on a Sunday for what he did on Saturday and is going to do on Monday.'

Ambrose Bierce

Religion

Don't start me on religion. Every man and his dog has an opinion nowadays, including the atheists, and none of them can keep it to themselves. They can't all be right. Some estimates reckon there are over 4,000 different religions in the world. I think the Greeks and the Romans and the Vikings had the right idea – loads of different gods for different things, and if you wanted to worship one of them more than the others, good luck to you. Live and let live, I say. Don't these religious types realise that all most of us want is to be left alone? I had a Jehovah's Witness at the door the other day, he said the Lord wanted everything made clean, but when I offered him a sponge and a bucket and said he could make a start on my car he soon disappeared. I don't know what to make of it all, to be honest, but when you get to my age you do start hedging your bets. As that Frenchman said on his deathbed when he was asked to renounce the Devil, this is no time to be making new enemies.

What do you call a sleep-walking nun?
A Roaming Catholic.

First old git: I've just bought some Armageddon cheese.
Second old git: What do you mean?
First old git: Well, it just says, 'Best Before End...'

What happened when Moses went to Mount Olive?
Popeye kicked his teeth in.

Vicar: I hope you never entertain lewd thoughts, Mr Perkins.
Perkins: No, vicar, I let them entertain me.

> Jesus loves you — everyone else thinks you're a grumpy old git.

How does a rabbi make a cup of tea?

Hebrews it.

A nun is in the shower when there's a knock on the bathroom door.

'Who is it?' she asks, stepping out of the shower.

'It's the blind man.'

Ah, that's OK, she thinks.

So she opens the door and the man says, 'Where do you want your blind?'

Teacher: What's the difference between the Old Testament and the New Testament?

Jimmy: Is the New Testament the Kindle version?

Two bishops were talking about the terrible lapse in moral standards.

'I never slept with my wife before we were married,' said the first bishop, 'did you?'

'I'm not sure,' said his companion, 'what was her maiden name?'

A Buddhist went into Subway and asked, 'Make me one with everything.'

The assistant gave him his Sub, the Buddhist gave him a £20 note and it went straight in the till.

'Where's my change?' he asked.

'Ah,' said the assistant, 'change comes from within.'

A vicar started his sermon: 'Today's sermon is about the sin of lying. Put your hands up if you read St Mark's gospel, chapter 17, like I asked you to last week.'

Half the congregation's hands went up. 'Right,' said the vicar, 'all you with your hands up had better listen extra carefully – St Mark's gospel only has 16 chapters.'

What happens if you don't pay your exorcist?
Your house gets repossessed.

A old git who was obviously drunk was reading a paper on the Tube when a priest got on. 'Father,' he asked, 'what causes arthritis?'

Seeing a chance to frighten the man into sober habits, the priest said, 'It's usually the result of excessive drinking and a debauched lifestyle. How long have you had it?'

'Oh, I don't have it. But it says here that the Pope has.'

Two old gits, Horace and Herbert, were in a pub and Horace was convinced the man at the next table was the Archbishop of Canterbury, but Herbert said it wasn't. In the end they had a £20 bet on it.

They went up to the man and Horace began, 'Excuse me, we were just wondering…'

'Leave me alone or I'll glass you!' shouted the man.

As they went back to their table, Horace said, 'That's a shame, I don't suppose we'll ever find out now…'

Vicar: I went past your house yesterday, Mr Smith.

Smith: Thank you very much, Vicar.

'Television is called a medium because when something is well done it's rare.'

Fred Allen

TV and Entertainment

TV used to be great when we all sat in one room and watched it together: Dad's Army, Starsky and Hutch, Morecambe and Wise, Police 5 with Shaw Taylor for a bit of a thrill. And even if it was rubbish, we still all watched it because there was nothing else to do: Love Thy Neighbour, MacMillan and Wife, Seaside Special ... God, they were awful. But because we all watched it at the same time, the next day we could have a chat about how terrible it was. If you missed it, you missed it – no video, no DVD, no catch-up. Then there were three channels broadcasting from 4pm to midnight and it was still full of rubbish. So with hundreds of channels nowadays on 24 hours a day, it's just as well there are hundreds of times more talented people around today than there were then ... oh, hang on a minute, THERE AREN'T! No wonder half the channels today are showing what people were watching an hour ago. What I want is TV an hour in front, so I can watch the racing and then get a bet on...

Why is watching Channel 5 like cooking a rare steak?

After two minutes you have to turn it over.

A young actor landed his first part, albeit a small one. All he had to do was go on stage with a rose, hold it to his nose and say, 'Ah, the sweet fragrance of my lover.'

He practised and practised for weeks and on the first night he delivered the line perfectly, only to go off stage for the director to shout at him, 'You moron! You've ruined the play!'

'But I didn't forget the line,' said the puzzled actor.

'No, but you forgot the rose!'

There was a big surprise on X Factor last night.

There were only 12 advert breaks.

I used to do Eric Morecambe impersonations, but now I've seen the error of my wa-heys!

Old git at theatre: Was it your toes I trod on when I went for the ice creams?
Lady: Yes, it was.
Old git: Good, I'm in the right row.

Why couldn't Ronnie Corbett play poker with Bruce Forsyth?
Brucie brought the cards and Ronnie couldn't hold them in his hands.

First old git: Was that show you went to see any good?
Second old git: It was so bad they were giving us our money back on the way in.

First Elizabethan: Are you going to see Henry IV Part II?

Second Elizabethan: No, I'm fed up of sequels.

Who's the most famous presenter on Australian television?

Louis the Roo.

How did the world's worst director shoot two films at the same time?

It was his first and his last.

How do you drown an actress?

Put a mirror at the bottom of her swimming pool.

Useless conjuror: For my next trick, I shall require an egg.

Old git: Believe me, if any of us had one you'd have had it by now.

How many sound engineers does it take to change a light bulb?
One, two... one, two...

A man appearing as Hamlet was being booed for his performance. Eventually he snapped.
'Don't blame me,' he shouted. 'I didn't write this rubbish.'

What happened to the terrible young stand-up on his first night?
His mother egged him on and the audience egged him off.

First old git: I watched a documentary on marijuana last night.
Second old git: Was it any good?
First old git: Well, I think it was about railways, but I was so stoned I can't remember.

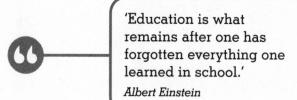

'Education is what remains after one has forgotten everything one learned in school.'

Albert Einstein

Education

Education in this country is in a right state, thanks chiefly to politicians of the left and right. Firstly, they've realised that continually raising the school-leaving age and shipping people off to take degrees in origami keeps them off the unemployment register for a few more years. When most kids left school at 14, was the nation full of illiterate knuckle-draggers? No, we showed Hitler what he could do with his plans for a new living room. When only five per cent of people went to university, were we desperately importing foreigners to invent the jet engine and the hovercraft and the automatic kettle? Exactly. Secondly, every few minutes the politicians change the curriculum and the exam system, so no kid gets the same education as anybody else. This permanent changing of the goalposts is supposedly to improve standards, but in actual fact is intended to make it impossible to judge one school generation against another, so every government can claim to be making things better. It almost makes you feel sorry for the little brats in education.

First old git: My son's studied the violin for years, you know.

Second old git: Is he any good?

First old git: He's just about worked out that it's a musical instrument made of wood and string.

What's the difference between a university student and ET?

ET phoned home.

Teacher: Jimmy, if you have £1.34 and you ask your Dad for £2.50, how much will you have?

Jimmy: £1.34, miss.

Teacher: I can see you don't know your mental arithmetic.

Jimmy: And I can see you don't know my Dad.

What does the national grammar champion win?

A posh trophy.

> **Did you hear about the poor old git who was illiterate and ambidextrous?**
>
> He couldn't write with both hands.

Teacher (pointing at Jimmy): At the end of this ruler is a complete idiot.

Jimmy: Which end, sir?

Teacher: Where did you go on holiday, Jimmy?

Jimmy: We went to Kirkcudbright, miss.

Teacher: And how do you spell that place?

Jimmy: Actually, now I come to think about it, we went to Dundee.

Teacher: How can you prove that the Earth is round, Jimmy?

Jimmy: I never said it was, miss.

Teacher: Ronnie, this essay on your cat is the same, word for word, as your brother wrote for me in this class last year.

Ronnie: Yes, miss, it's the same cat.

Son: Dad, can I take that pork pie round to Gran's?

Dad: I suppose so, but why?

Son: My maths teacher says for homework tonight we've got to take pie to one dismal place.

Teacher: What is a synonym?

Jane: Miss, is it a word you use when you can't spell the word you want to use?

Two old political philosophers are sitting in a nudist camp.

One says, 'Have you read Marx?'

'Yes,' replies the other, 'it must be these wicker chairs.'

How do you comfort an upset English teacher?
There, their, they're.

How can you spot a chemistry student in the toilets?
They wash their hands on the way in.

First atom: Did you hear oxygen is going out with magnesium?
Second atom: OMg!

Jimmy: My teacher must be hundreds of years old.
Johnny: Why?
Jimmy: He told us he taught Shakespeare at his last school.

Teacher: Stonehenge is over 4,000 years old.
Jimmy: That's impossible, miss – it's only 2014 now.

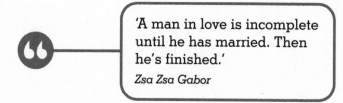

'A man in love is incomplete until he has married. Then he's finished.'

Zsa Zsa Gabor

Marriage

Marriage, as they say, is an institution, but who wants to live in an institution for 40 years? The Mormons had the right idea: a different wife for every day of the week, then nobody gets bored. And I'm not sexist – if women want a different hubby every day, that's fine by me too. I'm sure there's an app somewhere now that could sort out all the logistics to make sure Wife 3 didn't cook me the same tea as Wife 4 had the day before. I could have a weekend wife who's good at putting her own shelves up (or, even better, has a weekend job), and Mrs Old-Git could have a weekend husband who enjoys mowing the lawn. With a regular change of partner nobody will get sick of anybody, so divorce rates will come down, and with a bit of luck none of them will be able to keep track of what they've made me promise to do around the house.

Traffic policeman: I've been trying to get you to pull over for ages. Your wife fell out of the back of your car five miles back.

Old git: Thank goodness for that, I thought I'd gone deaf.

What's the longest sentence in the English language?

I do.

Old git's wife: Why haven't you bought me anything for my birthday?

Old git: Well, you know last year I bought you that nice plot in the cemetery you wanted?

Wife: Yes.

Old git: Well, you haven't used that yet.

First old git: Why have you given up drinking?
Second old git: Well, the other night I came home to my wife after a few pints and I saw two of her. Never again.

Sheila: Why did you have your husband's ashes put in an egg-timer?
Joyce: Well, I thought he might as well make himself useful for once.

Wife: You must be daft, running that electric fire all day. It'll cost you a fortune.
Old git: I'm not that stupid – I borrowed it from next door.

Wife: If you've got nothing to do, you could paint the front door ... there's plenty of paint in the loft.
Old git: Don't be daft, how am I going to get the door into the loft?

Old git: Is the steak tender?
Butcher: As tender as a woman's heart.
Old git: I'll have a pound of sausages, please.

Why are men like guns?
If you keep one around the house, eventually you'll want to shoot it.

Why is a book better than a woman?
You can shut a book up.

Old git: I sometimes think I'm my own worst enemy.
Wife: Not while I'm alive, you're not.

First old git: The police locked me up for throwing my wife's clothes out of the window.

Second old git: That seems a bit harsh.

First old git: Well, she was still wearing them at the time.

Old git: I suppose we should mark our golden wedding in some way.

Wife: How about having a two-minute silence?

Doris: Why do you say it wouldn't be fair to have a battle of wits with your husband?

Joan: Well, he's completely unarmed.

First old git: When me and my wife argue, she gets historical.

Second old git: Don't you mean hysterical?

First old git: No, she starts saying, 'I haven't forgotten what you did five years ago...'

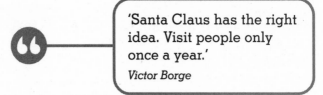

'Santa Claus has the right idea. Visit people only once a year.'
Victor Borge

Christmas

What is a grumpy old git to do when confronted with the open goal of a modern Christmas, that annual festival of goodwill to all men? People are queuing up to have a moan about how the true meaning of the season has been lost. So here's my two penn'orth.

Christmas these days is a ruddy disgrace. It's the one time of year we all get to take a few days off work and get completely hammered, and yet you can't move for moralising do-gooders telling you not to take Christ out of Christmas, and how it's not all about eating, drinking and presents.* Yes, it ruddy well is! What sort of hypocrite would I be to spend all year avoiding churches, only to pop in once a year when I know they'll be doling out the sherry and mince pies? 'Hello, Jesus, you might remember me from last year, I usually pop in on your birthday and drink all your booze, then ignore you for the next twelve months.' So, I hate Christmas because it's too religious, and the sooner we let M&S take over the C of E and run it properly, the better.

* Just make sure you include the receipts with mine so I can swap them after Christmas for something I actually want.

Jimmy: Granddad, can I have a dog for Christmas?

Old git: No, you'll have turkey like everyone else.

Patient: Doctor, I'm terrified of Father Christmas.

Doctor: Ah, you've got Claustrophobia.

Why is Christmas just like another day at the office?

You do all the work and the fat guy in the suit gets all the credit.

How does Father Christmas climb back up the chimney?

He uses a ladder in the stocking.

What do you give a reindeer with an upset stomach?

Elk-a-seltzer.

What's the substitute called in Santa's helpers' cricket team?
The twelf man.

What do you a female elf

A shelf.

Dad: I thought I told you to go and clear the snow?
Son: That's where I'm going.
Dad: But you've only got one welly on.
Son: That's OK, there's only one foot of snow.

How do we know Santa has passed his driving test?
There are Noel plates on his sleigh.

Santa's sleigh broke down so he flagged down a passing car for help.
'Sorry,' said the motorist, 'I'm not a mechanic, I'm a chiropodist.'
'Well,' said Santa, 'could you give me a toe?'

is a broken drum the best Christmas
 sent?
can't beat it.

Teacher: Name one of Santa's reindeer, apart
from Rudolph.
Jimmy: Olive, the rude one, miss.
Teacher: I don't think that's right.
Jimmy: Yes it is: 'Olive, the other reindeer, used to
laugh and call him names...'

What's brown and creeps round the house at
Christmas?
Mince spies.

What's the difference between snowmen and snow-women?
Snowballs.

First old git: I've just saved myself a fortune.
Second old git: How did you do that?
First old git: I went outside at midnight and let off my shotgun. Then this morning I told the kids Santa had committed suicide.

What nationality is Father Christmas?
North Polish.

How does Good King Wenceslas like his pizza?
Deep-pan, crisp and even.

> Dad: Christmas is cancelled this year.
>
> Son: Why?
>
> Dad: Because in your letter to Santa you said you'd been good, and he died laughing.

Why is Santa having to work extra hard this year?
The elves won the Euromillions jackpot in November.

Jimmy: Dad, why have you just given me loads of batteries this year?
Dad: Can't you see the note? It says 'Toys not included'.

Who wakes you up on Christmas Eve with a plate of macaroni?
The Ghost of Christmas Pasta.

The staff at the postal sorting office see a letter just addressed to Santa and open it. It's a note from a little old lady, saying she's so hard up she can't afford £50 to buy her grandchildren Christmas presents. Touched, the staff have a whip-round and raise £40, which they put in an envelope and post back to her. A few days later there is another letter to Santa in the same handwriting, and they open it.

'Dear Santa,' it reads, 'thank you so much for sending me the money I needed. Unfortunately it was ten pounds short – I expect it was those thieving gits at the Post Office.'

Patient: Doctor, I think I'm allergic to Christmas decorations.
Doctor: Sounds like tinselitis to me.

How do you scare a snowman?
With a hairdryer.

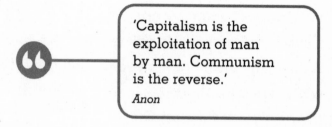

'Capitalism is the exploitation of man by man. Communism is the reverse.'

Anon

Politicians

Where do I start? Do you want to vote for the party that will take all your money and mess up the economy, or the party that will mess up the economy and take all your money? Or the party that gets the least votes but decides which of the other two pillocks gets to mess things up? All of them are led by a person who is convinced there is no one, absolutely no one, who knows more than them about running the country. Would you want an egomaniac like that in charge of anything? About 99 per cent of politicians are ambitious gits who decided at university that a career in politics would be better than working for a living, and then had to choose which party would give them the best chance of succeeding. No principles at all. But the ones you really want to watch out for are the one per cent who believe in what they say, and really like the idea of bossing other people around. And if you are thinking of putting an x next to any of their names, remember: whoever you vote for, the Government always gets in.

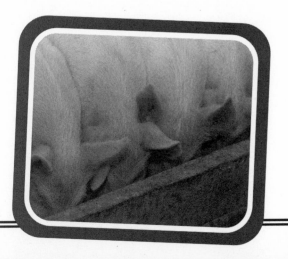

What's the difference between democracy and feudalism?

With democracy, your vote counts; with feudalism your count votes.

What's the difference between an Airfix model and a politician?

One is a glueless kit...

Local councillor: I think it would be good for tourism if we bought a gondola for the town pool. Second councillor: I've got a better idea. If we spend a bit more money and buy a pair they can breed.

Suppose you were photographing the Niagara Falls and George Osborne falls in and is swept past. You can either save him or take the picture of a lifetime. So here's the tricky question: What shutter speed should you use?

The British Society of Anarchists' AGM ended successfully yesterday when no one could call the meeting to order.

An old git is stuck in a traffic jam in London when a policeman knocks on his window.

Old git: What's up?

Policeman: An armed gang has invaded Parliament and has all the MPs hostage. They say if they don't get ten million pounds they'll douse them all with petrol and set fire to them. We're going from car to car making a collection.

Old git: How much have most people been giving?

Policeman: About a gallon.

What's the difference between the Government and the Mafia?

One of them is organised.

A vicar went to get his hair cut and when he went to pay the barber said, 'No charge, it's a service to the Lord.' The next day he found a dozen prayer books on his doorstep as a thank you.

A week later the local baker went to the same barber and was given a free cut: 'It's a service to our community.' The next day he found a dozen cakes on his doorstep.

A week later an MP went to have his hair cut and the barber said: 'No charge, it's a service to our country.' The next day he found a dozen MPs on his doorstep.

Old git: Can I speak to my MP?

Secretary: I'm afraid he died last week. Who's calling?

Old git: Albert Perkins.

Secretary: Hang on, what's your game? You've rung up five times already this week and every time I've told you the same: Your MP died last week.

Old git: I know, I just love hearing you say it.

A Conservative candidate rings on the door of a house. There is no answer. He knocks. No answer. He knocks again, much harder. Finally a man answers the door.

'Do you realise I work night shifts? And you've just woken up the baby! And now my wife is screaming at me! What the hell do you want? It had better be important.'

Thinking quickly, the budding politician says, 'I'm sorry, sir, I'm your Labour candidate and I'd just like to know if I can rely on your vote...'

Policeman: What are you burying in that ditch with your tractor?

Farmer: Well, a minibus full of politicians overturned half an hour ago and they were all killed, so I'm burying them before the flies can get at them.

Policeman: Hang on, are you sure they were all dead?

Farmer: Well, one or two said they weren't, but you know what liars these politicians are...

Nick Clegg goes into the bank to withdraw some cash and is asked for ID, which he hasn't got.
'Perhaps you could do something to prove who you are?' suggests the cashier.
'What do you mean?' asks Clegg.
'Well, for example, if you were Andy Murray you could show us a perfect serve. If you were Gareth Bale you could show us how to take a perfect free kick.'
Clegg ponders for a minute. 'It's no use, I can't think of a single thing I'm good at.'
'Would you like tens or twenties, Mr Clegg?'

Why is politics so named?
From 'poly' meaning 'many' and 'ticks' meaning 'bloodsucking creatures'.

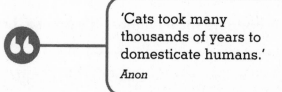

'Cats took many thousands of years to domesticate humans.'

Anon

𝒫ets

Now you may be thinking, 'We've already had a section on animals – why do we need a section on pets as well?' There is a simple and logical answer: I had too many jokes about animals to fit in one section. So ... what is it about this country that makes people go potty over pets? Billions of pounds spent on expensive fancy-tasting dog and cat food to give to animals who lick their own bums! Millions of pounds left in people's wills to animal charities, when there are plenty of miserable old gits out there whose lives would be made a little brighter with some of that money. And I happen to know the old lady down the street from me spends enough in one week on nuts and seeds for the birds in her garden to keep me in Capstan Ready Rubbed for a month. The world's gone mad...

A cat is in the garden one night when he bumps into a gnome.

'What on earth are you?' asks the cat.

'I'm a gnome,' says the gnome. 'I steal food, mess up the garden and make funny noises all night long to keep people awake. Why, what are you?' he asks the cat.

'Erm ... I must be a gnome.'

If your wife is shouting to be let in at the front and your dog is barking to be let in at the back, which do you let in first?

The dog, because he'll shut up when you let him in.

Police say they are having difficulty identifying illegal dangerous dogs accurately. I don't see the problem. If they've got short legs, square shoulders and an aggressive temperament, then the dog they own is most likely illegal.

> **What happened when the man sold his three-legged retriever on eBay?**
>
> It didn't fetch very much.

First old git: Our dog's been missing four days now.
Second old git: Why don't you put a notice in the local paper?
First old git: Don't be daft, he can't read.

Old git: I want to return this golden retriever.
Pet shop owner: Why what's the problem?
Old git: It hasn't found a thing. I knew I should have bought a metal detector in the first place.

First old git: I was thrown out of the pet shop yesterday for making a parrot laugh.
Second old git: Blimey, that's polly-tickle correctness gone mad, that is.

An old git was sitting on a park bench eating a sandwich when a lady with a little dog sat down next to him. The dog kept pestering and pawing and whining to the old git for some food so eventually he said to the lady, 'Do you mind if I throw him a bit?'
'No,' she replied, so the old git picked up the dog and threw him over the hedge.

What do you get if you cross a dog with a monkey?
Prosecuted by the RSPCA.

An Alsatian and a dachshund are walking through a snowy field.
'My feet are freezing,' says the Alsatian.
'Think yourself lucky,' replies the dachshund.

What do you call a dog that can find anything?
A Labragoogle.

What should you do if you steal a pet rabbit?

Make a run for it.

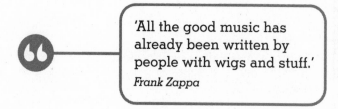

'All the good music has
already been written by
people with wigs and stuff.'
Frank Zappa

Music

Music is so ruddy awful nowadays. Every Tom, Dick or Harriet thinks they can be a pop star if they've got enough of a sob story to get on X Factor, and most of them have got a voice like a squirrel being strangled by a length of knicker elastic impregnated with razor blades. Or else there are bands that so far as I can see consist of one lead singer who's tone deaf, one keyboardist wearing mittens, one guitarist who can't tune his instrument and one drummer with no rhythm. And, best of all, they write their own songs. And do I have to mention rap? It is to music what Eric Pickles is to ballet dancing. But at least modern pop music is trying to sound musical. Modern classical music is like modern art – anyone who doesn't like it obviously doesn't understand what the composer is trying to achieve. But I understand – they are trying to extract the maximum amount of urine for the minimum amount of talent, funded by us via the Arts Council. Where's John Cage and his 4½ minutes of silence when you need him?

First old git: I found a ticket for a rap music concert nailed to a tree the other day, so I took it.
Second old git: You never did?
First old git: Course I did. You never know when you might need a nail.

First old git: Have you heard that new band, 'Duvet'?
Second old git: No.
First old git: They're a cover band.

Bob Geldof was at Live Aid, and said, 'Every time I clap my hands a child dies.'
'Stop ruddy clapping, then,' somebody shouted from the crowd.

What's the difference between a conductor and God?

God doesn't think he's a conductor.

What's the difference between terrorists and accordion players?

Terrorists have sympathisers.

What do you call a beautiful woman on a trombonist's arm?

A tattoo.

What's the difference between a drummer and a vacuum cleaner?

One of them needs plugging in before it sucks.

What do you call a drummer in a suit?

The defendant.

What's the definition of perfect pitch?
When you throw a banjo into a skip and it hits an accordion.

Why are a violinist's fingers like lightning?
They rarely strike the same spot twice.

What's the difference between a tuba player and a bag of rubbish?
The bag of rubbish gets taken out once a week.

Why are harps like ageing parents?
Both are unforgiving and hard to get in and out of the car.

What's the difference between a dead squirrel in the road and a dead trombonist in the road?
It's just possible that the squirrel was on his way to a gig.

Why are concert intervals limited to 20 minutes?
So they don't have to retrain the drummer.

What happens if you play country music backwards?
Your wife returns to you, your dog comes back to life and you get let out of prison.

What's the definition of opera?
A play in which, if someone gets stabbed, instead of bleeding he sings.

What's the definition of an intellectual?
Someone who can listen to the William Tell Overture without thinking of the Lone Ranger.

What's the definition of an alto?
A soprano who can sight-read.

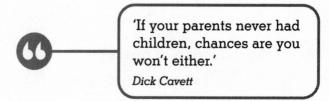

'If your parents never had
children, chances are you
won't either.'
Dick Cavett

Children

I know that we have to have kids. Otherwise, who else is going to work so that my pension can be paid and my nursing home can afford Sky in a few years' time? Once they grow up and start paying tax, I'll admit they can be quite useful. But why do we have to have that 20-year period before they contribute anything to society? They start out smelly, noisy and incapable of doing anything for themselves and it just goes downhill from there. Millions of pains in the bum wandering around giving me funny looks in their hoodies while I'm standing at the bus stop glaring at them from inside my balaclava. And the well-behaved ones are even worse. Have you seen the little robots on programmes like Young Musician of the Year (BBC4), Young Plumber of the Decade (BBC2) and Young Drug-dealer of the Century (BBC3)? Groomed to within an inch of their lives, butter wouldn't melt in their mouths. You just know it's only a few years before they're knocking on your door pestering you for your vote, or to buy the Watchtower, or to fill out a standing order for Save the Wombat – I've been mugged and chugged in my time, and there's not much to choose between them,
believe me.

> Mum: Don't cry, Sally, you know
> Dad had to drown the kittens.
>
> Sally: Yes, but he promised I could do it.

First old git: I hope my new grandson will be all right, he only weighed four pounds at birth.
Second old git: Don't worry, I didn't weigh that much when I was born.
First old git: And did you live?
Second old git: Course I did. You should see me now.

Six-year-old Jane came home and asked her mum, 'Where do I come from?'
Jane's mum was quite progressive and believed in being straight with her children, so she gave Jane a simplified but graphic description of the facts of life.
'Thanks, Mum,' said Jane. 'I only asked because there's a new girl in our class and she says she comes from Wales.'

Grandson: This egg's a bad one.

Granddad: Shut up and eat it up.

Grandson: Have I got to eat the beak and legs as well?

Jimmy is eating his tea when he stretches over the table to reach for the jam.

'Haven't you got a tongue?' asks his Dad.

'Yes,' says Jimmy, 'but it isn't long enough.'

Granddad: You ought to pay more attention, young man. Let me tell you why. 'A wise old owl sat in an oak, The more he heard the less he spoke, The less he spoke the more he heard, Why can't we all be like that wise old bird?' Now, what do you think of that?

Granddad: Sorry, I stopped listening after '… sat in an oak'.

An old git watched a young boy stuffing his face with chocolate bar after chocolate bar in the park. On the sixth one he couldn't contain himself. Going over to him, he said, 'You know, eating all that chocolate will give you acne, make you fat and rot your teeth.'

'Is that so?' said the boy. 'Well my granddad lived to be ninety-seven.'

'And did he eat six chocolate bars a day?'

'No, he minded his own ruddy business.'

Jimmy: A bishop came to our school today.

Mum: And what did he say?

Jimmy: Not much, but at least now I know what a crook looks like.

Jimmy: I'm glad you decided to call me Jimmy.

Dad: That's nice, but why?

Jimmy: Because that's what everyone at school calls me.

Jimmy: My Dad fell in the well last night, miss.

Teacher: Oh dear, is he all right?

Jimmy: I think he must be – he'd stopped calling for help by this morning, anyway.

A salesman knocked on the door of a house and it was answered by a ten-year-old boy smoking a cigarette and holding a pint of beer.

'Excuse me,' said the salesman, 'but is your mother in?'

Taking a puff and a swig, the boy said, 'What do you think?'

'Margaret Thatcher will never speak well on television. Her impulse to tell the microphone to pull itself together is too great.'

Edward Pearce

Ask Your Granddad

A lot of jokes nowadays aren't really jokes as I'd think of them. They're witticisms, clever remarks to show how smart people are, or how offensive they can be. I've got nothing against being offensive per se, I seem to spend a fair bit of time doing it myself; I'm just amazed they get so many people to pay a fortune to go to a vast arena to watch a stand-up perform his routine on a giant telly. It's a bit different from Colin Crompton holding court at The Wheeltappers and Shunters Social Club. A good joke, however, can stand the test of time. When Adam said to Eve, 'That's a lovely pear you've got there,' and Eve replied, 'I think you'll find it's an apple,' and Adam said, 'I know a lovely pear when I see one,' God was writing a joke that would still be funny 6,000 years later. But some gags are quite specific to their era, so here are a few that might have the younger reader searching Google to find out why they're funny, after which they won't be funny any more. Never mind...

First old git: You know this brain drain that's supposed to be going on?
Second old git: Yes.
First old git: Can you think of a single politician we've lost?

They're going to remake On the Buses and set it in space.
It'll be called Blakey's Seven.

The lead singer of the Flying Pickets has been taken to hospital with suspected food poisoning. When asked what caused it a spokesman said, 'Bad ham, bad ham...'

Why do Austin Allegros have heated rear windows?

To keep your hands warm when you're pushing it.

> **I've just seen Lee Majors and he looks a million dollars ... he's really let himself go.**

America has Ronald Reagan, Johnny Cash, Bob Hope and Stevie Wonder.
Britain has Margaret Thatcher, no cash, no hope ... and no wonder.

How do you double the value of an Austin Allegro?
Fill it with petrol.

Russian television has just launched a second channel. So if you get fed up of the speeches of Leonid Brezhnev on Channel 1, just turn to Channel 2 where there's a KGB officer pointing a gun saying, 'Turn back to Channel 1.'

What's the definition of a string quartet?
The Moscow Symphony Orchestra returning from
a tour of the USA.

**Brian Clough, Bob Paisley and Ron Greenwood all
die and go to heaven. God welcomes them on his
throne and asks them, by way of an entrance
exam, to tell him a little of what they believe.**
Ron Greenwood says, 'I believe I made a difference
to English football; as England manager I got to the
World Cup finals and we always played very fairly.'
**'All right,' says God, 'you can come and sit on my
left hand.'**
Bob Paisley says, 'I believe I put English club
football on the map. My Liverpool team conquered
Europe and set a great example to everyone.'
**'All right,' says God, who has a soft spot for
football, 'you can come and sit on my right hand.
What about you, Mr Clough?'**
'I believe you're sitting in my chair.'

A man goes to the barber and asks for a Tony Curtis cut. The barber shaves his head so he's completely bald.

When the man sees what he's done he says, 'You idiot, do you know who Tony Curtis is?'

'I should do, I watch Kojak every week.'

Why did they call Frank Carson 'Sinbad'?

He was the thief of bad gags.

Motorist: Can you change the oil in my Austin Allegro?

Mechanic: If I were you I'd keep the oil and change the car.

What did Harry Corbett say to his hand?

Sooty, put some clothes on!

'He may look like an idiot
and talk like an idiot, but
don't let that fool you –
he really is an idiot.'

Groucho Marx

Idiots

There are a lot of jokes about idiots, but then there are a hell of a lot of idiots about. Jokes would have you believe that there are a greater proportion of idiots among certain populations – blondes, Irish people, footballers, Brummies – so I won't disappoint you by not using these stereotypes. But in my experience you can never tell who's going to ruin your day by their thickness. It might be that twerp in front of you at the Post Office with a dozen parcels who needs the six different delivery options explaining for each one; or the fool in the car at the traffic lights who doesn't see the lights change for the feeder lane until just before they turn back to red again; or perhaps it's the chump who leaves your parcel in your wheelie bin 'for safety' without letting you know. So if I was going to use a shorthand for idiots based on my own experience, it would have to be 'practically everybody who crosses my path in the course of an average day', which isn't very snappy. Blondes it is, then...

How did the footballer die raking leaves?
He fell out of the tree.

First Brummie: There's a new car wash opened just down the road from you.
Second Brummie: Great, I'll be able to walk there.

What happened when the idiot shot an arrow in the air?
He missed.

Old git at bar: Do you want to hear a blonde joke?
Barmaid: I ought to tell you, underneath this hat I'm blonde. You may not have noticed but there's a blonde either side of you. And I'll call my boss over to hear it if you like, because she's blonde too. Now, do you still want to tell your blonde joke?
Old git: Now you put it like that, no. Not if I'm going to have to explain it four times.

First old git: Why are you pulling that piece of string?
Second old git: You ought to try pushing it!

What do you call an intelligent blonde?

A golden retriever.

Brunette: Are you going to eat that banana?

Blonde: Yes, as soon as I can find the zip.

Brummie: Have I missed the No. 12 bus?

Man at bus stop: Yes, it's just left.

Brummie: Never mind, I'll catch the No. 24 and get off halfway.

Grandma: I know how to make your granddad's eyes light up.

Granddaughter: How?

Grandma: Shine a torch in his ear.

> **How do blondes' brain cells die?**
>
> Alone.

What did the idiot say when the aeroplane went through turbulence?
'Oh my God, an earthquake!'

What happened to the blonde fox that was stuck in a trap?
She chewed off three legs and was still stuck.

Brummie: I'd like a potato clock, please.
Jeweller: I've never heard of one, sir. We sell cuckoo clocks, grandfather clocks, wall clocks, but not potato clocks. Are you sure that's what you need?
Brummie: Definitely. I start a new job tomorrow at nine o'clock, and my wife said, 'You'd better get a potato clock.'

What happened to the Irish inventor?
He went bankrupt after launching his solar-powered torch.

A footballer is fed up of not getting upgrades on aeroplanes, so on his next trip to New York he goes and sits in first class and refuses to move. Several stewards try to persuade him to leave, but he won't. Finally a stewardess goes and whispers to him and he immediately goes back to his proper seat.

'What did you say to him?' ask the stewards.

'I told him first class didn't stop in New York.'

The Irish programme to launch a rocket into space has been postponed until they can find a big enough milk bottle.